CHIEF ILLINIWEK

A TRIBUTE TO AN ILLINOIS TRADITION

The News-Gazette®

SportsPublishingLLC.com

The News-Gazette®

John Foreman, **EDITOR AND PUBLISHER,**
THE CHAMPAIGN-URBANA NEWS-GAZETTE

Jim Turpin
Loren Tate
Tom Kacich

Jim Dey
Amy Eckert
Jodi Heckel

THE CHAMPAIGN-URBANA NEWS-GAZETTE PHOTO DEPARTMENT:

Darrell Hoemann, **PHOTO EDITOR**
Vanda Bidwell
Heather Coit
Rick Danzl

John Dixon
Holly Hart
Robert O'Daniell
Robin Scholz

PUBLISHERS: Peter L. Bannon and Joseph J. Bannon Sr.
SENIOR MANAGING EDITOR: Susan M. Moyer
ACQUISITIONS EDITOR: Noah Amstadter
DEVELOPMENTAL EDITOR: Laura E. Podeschi
PHOTO EDITOR: Erin Linden-Levy
ART DIRECTOR: K. Jeffrey Higgerson
COVER DESIGN: K. Jeffrey Higgerson
GRAPHIC DESIGNER: Dustin J. Hubbart

ISBN 13: 978-1-59670-280-6

Front cover photo: Dan Maloney by John Dixon/The Champaign-Urbana News-Gazette
Back cover photos (clockwise from top): Matt Veronie by Darrell Hoemann/The Champaign-Urbana News-Gazette; Ben Forsyth by Dennis Trumble/Champaign-Urbana Courier, Courtesy of the Champaign County Historical Archive, The Urbana Free Library; Scott Christensen (left) with Chief Frank Fools Crow provided by The Champaign-Urbana News-Gazette; Idelle Stith Brooks by Harold Holmes/The Champaign-Urbana News Gazette, Courtesy of the Champaign County Historical Archive, The Urbana Free Library; John Creech from the collection of Jean Edwards; Matt Gawne provided by The Champaign-Urbana News-Gazette

All interior photos provided by The Champaign-Urbana News-Gazette unless otherwise noted.

Multiple attempts have been made to properly credit the source of all photographs. The publishers regret any errors or omissions. In the event of mistaken attribution please notify the publisher for correction in any subsequent editions.

Printed in the United States of America.

Sports Publishing L.L.C.
804 North Neil Street
Champaign, IL 61820
Phone: 1-877-424-2665
Fax: 217-363-2073

CONTENTS

EDITOR'S NOTE

BY JOHN FOREMAN

On the wintry evening of February 21, 2007, Chief Illiniwek Dan Maloney took the floor of the University of Illinois Assembly Hall to thunderous ovation, just as he had many times before, performing the athletic twists, turns and leaps that—with small variations throughout time—have characterized thousands of performances by Chief Illiniwek over the years. It prompted the same enthusiasm it had prompted since a young student named Lester Leutwiler first performed it in 1926.

But this time, as nearly every seat in the Assembly Hall remained full, it also prompted tears.

And when Dan Maloney completed the dance and exited the floor, he did something no one could remember Chief Illiniwek ever doing before. He re-entered the arena, walked slowly to center court and offered a deliberate ceremonial gesture to each corner of the packed hall, slowly raising his hands toward the sky, then down toward the earth and finally in toward his heart. Observers likened it to a traditional Native American gesture sometimes called a prayer to the four winds, but Maloney said later that it was simply a very personal way of saying thank you to those who had given the Chief such support and energy over the years. He had discussed it beforehand only with his predecessors in the role.

So ended one of the most beloved traditions in all of collegiate athletic history. After years of controversy that had pitted determined activists against thousands of Illinois fans, students and alumni, the decision had been reached for Chief Illiniwek to dance no more.

This book isn't about that controversy. It doesn't rehash all the arguments or all the political gymnastics of a 20-year debate that took nearly as many twists and turns as Chief Illiniwek himself.

This book is about the tradition, the symbol, the spirit portrayed by young men (and one young woman) over the course of 81 years for the fans and alums who treasured those portrayals and all they represented. It documents the athleticism, sincerity and spirit of those young people, chronicles how the tradition was created and evolved and explains, in the words of many, the passion it evoked.

The Chief Illiniwek tradition was never simply about exciting the crowd at an athletic contest, although that surely was accomplished. It was always intended as a gesture of respect and affection for the University of Illinois and the Native American culture that preceded the university here. While some could never understand that, it was always quite clear to the students who portrayed Chief Illiniwek and the thousands who shared, some way, in what has come to be called "the Spirit of the Illini."

When Lester Leutwiler took the field in a costume he put together himself for what was supposed to be a one-time stunt involving an Indian dance, those who gave wit-

lege life at Illinois. It is one of many remarkable stories that followed the Chief over the years.

For the most part, this book represents the work of the staff at *The Champaign-Urbana News-Gazette*. I'm particularly grateful for the contributions of Amy Eckert, who hurriedly helped collect and assemble the pieces of this remarkable history, and to Karen Czerechowicz, who helped get the material in shape for publication. Loren Tate, the dean of all Big Ten sportswriters, contributed help and ideas, including an essay that attempts to describe how the great Illini Nation feels about its Chief. Tom Kacich, Jim Dey, Jim Turpin and a marvelous group of photographers over the years made major contributions.

Special thanks also go to Roger Huddleston and Jean Edwards, two remarkable people who have done more than anyone over the years to preserve and honor the tradition of Chief Illiniwek. This book is dedicated to them, as well as to all the great Illini who portrayed the Chief over the years. It must also be dedicated to that great Spirit of the Illini, evoked and celebrated in every performance of Chief Illiniwek.

It endures still in a million hearts.

John Foreman is editor and publisher of The Champaign-Urbana News-Gazette.

Chief Illiniwek John Madigan, 1998-2000.

> "It's not just an athletic symbol. It's the symbol of a great university."

Tom Livingston
Chief Illiniwek, 1988-89

THE SYMBOL OF THE UNIVERSITY OF ILLINOIS

By JIM TURPIN

It only took a moment.

A moment to tell the difference.

Some 60 years ago—when I saw Chief Illiniwek perform for the first time—I knew in a moment that I was witnessing something special.

This was not a mascot—dressed in a goofy costume—doing silly things on the sidelines. He was not a part of the cheerleaders, the dancing girls or the student cheering section. He did no fooling around with the opposing team's mascot; he didn't turn somersaults or cartwheels, like he belonged in the Macy's Thanksgiving Parade. He stood alone, a majestic figure who performed for four minutes, then disappeared ghostlike, not to be seen again until his next performance.

Chief Illiniwek has been the honored symbol of the University of Illinois for more than 80 years, recognized under state law as such. By formal action the U of I Board of Trustees declared him the symbol of the university. Studies, referenda and polls confirmed and reiterated the Chief as the official symbol of the University. Students who portray the Chief engage in extensive study and training to present a dignified and respectful performance.

Has Bucky Badger received such honors from the Wisconsin Legislature? Does the Florida State mascot—clad in loincloth, riding a horse and throwing a flaming spear—appear dignified and respectful? How much study and training does it take to suit up like a leprechaun and tippy-toe around the Golden Dome? Mascots are gophers, buckeyes, hawkeyes and badgers.

Only one university has a symbol: Chief Illiniwek.

When the Chief danced for the last time at the Illinois-Michigan basketball game, thousands stood and cheered. Many—both young and old—wiped away tears as the Chief left the court. Then, almost immediately, the U of I was hit

UI senior Brandon Bleess holds still as UI junior Megan Pfeffer paints a Chief logo onto his face before the home game Wednesday, February 21, 2007. Illinois beat Michigan 54-42.
John Dixon/The Champaign-Urbana News-Gazette

with an avalanche of phone calls, e-mails, letters, and petitions protesting that the Chief—as we have known him—is no more. Would this have been the reaction if a mascot had been fired? The answer is no. But this was no mascot. This was Chief Illiniwek.

How many former Bucky Badgers, for example, get together for reunions on a regular basis? The Council of Chiefs do. The men who portrayed Chief Illiniwek at the University of Illinois meet on a regular basis, they conference-call even more frequently; they are battling collectively to try to preserve the history and heritage of the symbol they love so much.

There was no tomahawk chopping when the Chief performed. Nobody beat on tom-toms. No disrespect was shown. Instead, students, alumni, little children and just plain Illini fans stood silently, arms folded, and waited respectfully until the Chief had left the arena. There would be an occasional "We love you Chief!" shouted by someone who was speaking for the group. Indeed, the Chief was—and is—loved by so many. That's why they hurt so much. It is not easy to give up someone you love. Many say that love will live on even though the Chief may dance no more.

Is there any such love for a mascot? Anywhere?

In fact, someone at the U of I Athletic Association had the idea a few years ago that the Illini needed a mascot. The Chief was great and would continue to do his halftime performances, but what we needed was a mascot. A person or thing that would run around the court and fire up the fans. He would do handsprings and playfully punch little kids in the nose. He would lead cheers, he would mug with the crowd and get his picture taken. He would be "one of those."

He was introduced one night at the Assembly Hall. He jumped out of a highly decorated box and began to run around the court like a crazy man, waving his arms and shouting to the crowd.

It only took a moment.

A moment to tell the difference.

The difference between a mascot and a symbol.

This character had all the characteristics of a mascot.

The crowd booed long and loud. The poor guy, who wasn't even dressed in orange and blue, put his head down and marched as quickly as possible out of the Assembly Hall.

In all the years that have followed, the U of I has never again tried to sell a mascot to the Illini Nation. The university would be wise to adhere to that policy in the future.

The Chief may never dance again, but the memory of this revered symbol will live on.

Mascots are a dime a dozen, but there is only one symbol.

Jim Turpin is a radio personality for WDWS-AM in Champaign and the longtime "Voice of the Fighting Illini."

Dan Maloney's last dance as Chief Illiniwek at Assembly Hall in Champaign, Illinois, on Wednesday, February 21, 2007.
John Dixon/The Champaign-Urbana News-Gazette

ORIGIN OF THE CHIEF

"Of all the symbols of the University, Chief Illiniwek most clearly evokes feelings of pride and dignity among students, alumni and friends.

"The Indians' appreciation of stewardship for all of nature, the Indians' humane understanding of community, and the Indians' deeply centered and grounded openness to the spiritual part of human beings, makes Chief Illiniwek an appropriate symbol for the University of Illinois community."

Notation beneath a portrait of the first Chief Illiniwek, Lester Leutwiler, displayed for many years at the University YMCA

Chief Illiniwek Gaylord "Dean" Spotts, 1953-1955.
From the collection of Jean Edwards

ILLINOIS INDIANS' TALE ONE OF PROSPERITY, PAIN

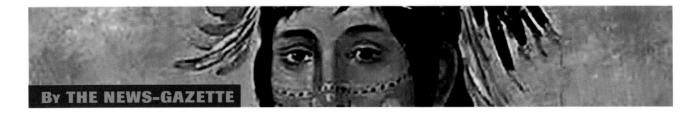

By THE NEWS-GAZETTE

Their name—actually a clumsy French interpretation of it—is virtually all that remains of the Illinois Indians who lived on these fertile prairies generations before white settlers.

The tribespeople were farmers and game hunters, savvy traders and sometime warriors—a highly developed and complex society of "gentle people," according to Europeans who knew them.

But in the end, the Illinois Indians met the same fate as dozens of other native peoples: Scarce in number and separated from their traditions, they all but dissolved and disappeared to a far-flung reservation.

The passionate controversy over the University of Illinois' Chief Illiniwek symbol dwells on questions of race and heritage. In the history of the real "Illini," however, the chief—if there ever was one—is barely a footnote.

The Illinois were some of the first Midwestern Indians to have sustained contact with the earliest white explorers in the region. These Indians built one of the oldest known settlements on the continent, the Grand Village of the Kaskaskia. And their sudden drop in population is still something of a mystery.

Their story, one anthropologist has said, is the place where "prehistory and history meet."

The Europeans rendered the group's name as "Illinois," which may have been a French pronunciation of an Indian word for "man." The name the Illinois had for themselves was the "insca," according to writings by the late Natalia Belting, a UI history professor.

"Illiniwek" is another form of the name given in the first French accounts, such as "Aliniouek" or "Iliniouec."

The Illinois Indians were a loosely organized band of independent tribes that spoke a single Algonquian language and inhabited a large territory the French writers called "Illinois Country," spanning most of the modern-day state.

Among the dozen or more tribes that initially made up the Illinois were Cahokia, the Tamaroa, the Michigamea, the Peoria and the Kaskaskia.

Pah-me-cow-ee-tah, "Man Who Tracks," a Peoria Indian chief from a painting by George Catlin.
Illinois Historical Survey collection

When white men met the Illinois for the first time, the French had laid claim to most territory west of the Appalachian Mountains.

Father Jacques Marquette, a Jesuit priest who ministered to Great Lakes Indians, wanted to establish a mission among the Illinois. In 1673, he accompanied Louis Jolliet, a young fur trader, on a foray to explore the Mississippi River.

Most of what historians and anthropologists know about the Illinois is based on eyewitness accounts left behind by Marquette and other explorers. Archaeology has yielded some additional clues.

The tribes had a mixed economy of hunting, gathering and gardening agriculture, experts believe.

The Illinois were a prosperous group, in part because they were for a time the undisputed owners of most of what is now the modern-day state, which enjoyed a central location for trade between the Great Lakes and the Mississippi and the expanding American West, said Duane Esarey, assistant curator for anthropology at the Illinois State Museum's Dickson Mounds site in Lewistown.

"The Illinois were in the middle. One reason they were so large and successful is they dominated trade" in furs and foodstuffs, Esarey said.

"They lived in big summer villages, conglomerations of several thousand people sometimes, from April to October or November. In winter, they split up into small groups and went all over the landscape, collecting furs and making a living off a more dispersed food base," he said.

Among the largest of those villages was the so-called Grand Village of the Kaskaskia, on the western bank of the Illinois River near Starved Rock. French explorers helped create what was then the largest Indian village in what is now the state of Illinois.

It was home to thousands of Indians whose tribes were included among the Illinois. Indians from throughout the region gathered at Kaskaskia to enjoy the protection of and to trade with the French colonists. Some anthropologists believe the site was inhabited as far back as 900 A.D.

In 1673, the Illinois were a large and powerful group that numbered 10,000 or 12,000 people. About 150 years later, they had been reduced to several hundred people—maybe as few as 80—and ceded the last of their lands to the United States.

"The big issue confronting the Illinois is their depopulation. That's an incredible decline," said Raymond Hauser, a history professor at Waubonsee Community College in Sugar Grove, who has written about the Illinois for 25 years.

Legend holds that the Illinois suffered a costly defeat in a war with the Iroquois at Starved Rock in the 17th century. Besieged on a rocky precipice by enemy warriors who would not let them come down, many Illinois starved to death.

Much of the legend is doubted by historians. Parts of it could be drawn from actual events, but the Illinois dwindled for a host of other reasons, too.

"It's kind of an interesting problem, but I don't know that the answers are that clear-cut. Certainly disease, alcoholism, absorption into the broader community" may have played a role, Esarey said. "The Illinois tribes weren't terribly conservative. They didn't keep their life way as close as other groups."

Hauser argues that the Illinois were doomed by their own willingness to become close to the French—and eventually depend on them.

"It was their greater dependency on Europeans that exposed them. They became more vulnerable," said Hauser.

Like other tribes, the Illinois suffered from deadly European diseases to which they had no immunity. Smallpox epidemics occurred in the region in about 1704, 1732 and 1756.

Dependence on the French powers slowly eliminated

the tribes' traditional ways of life. They were unable to provide for or defend themselves without help.

"It's not that the French were out to execute these people. The French encouraged close personal relationships. They intermarried with the Illinois," Hauer said.

The ultimate cause of the Illinois' decline was the colonial expansion of European nations. As France sought to establish a fur-trade empire in Canada, British colonies grew along the Atlantic seaboard and Spain established a foothold in the lower Mississippi Valley, according to Robert Warren, an associate curator of anthropology for the Illinois State Museum in Springfield.

"The Illini got caught in a vice that applied pressure to them from all directions. Warfare and disease caused massive depopulation, while the (dependency on the French) led to the abandonment of traditional ways of life," Warren wrote recently in an article.

The Illinois population became "precariously small" in the early 1800s. The Kaskaskia and Peoria tribes survived and settled on a joint reservation in eastern Kansas in 1832. They merged with the Wea and Piankashaw tribes in 1854. In 1867, they moved to a new reservation in northeast Oklahoma, Warren wrote.

The living descendants of the Illinois Indians are represented today by the Peoria Indian Tribe of Oklahoma, which maintains its tribal headquarters in Miami, Oklahoma, and currently has 2,650 members living throughout the United States.

Kee-mo-ra-nia, "No English," a Peoria Indian from a painting by George Catlin. *Illinois Historical Survey collection*

THE ORIGIN
OF CHIEF ILLINIWEK

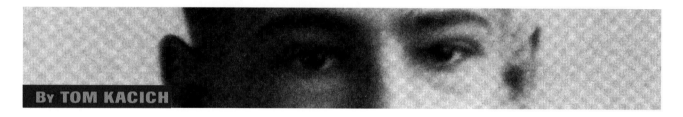

By TOM KACICH

If not for a band director from the University of Pennsylvania, a legendary football coach at the University of Illinois, an assistant band director at Illinois and a Boy Scout with an interest in Indian lore, the 81-year tradition of Chief Illiniwek never would have been born. That's the way Lester Leutwiler, a onetime Urbana Boy Scout, a 1929 University of Illinois graduate and the first Chief Illiniwek, remembered the tradition's origin.

"It was the fall of 1926," Leutwiler wrote in a brief, undated essay found in the UI Archives. "Knowing that the U. Of Penn. would be playing the Illini on October 30th, the Band Director from Penn called Ray Dvorak, Assistant Director of the U. of I. Marching Band to make plans for the halftime activities of the game.

"Ray was asked if he would get someone to represent the Illini—they would send a Wm. Penn suit for a band member to wear and represent the U. of Penn., which Ray agreed to do.

"Ray remembered that Indians lived in Illinois at one time. He also knew that I had made an Indian costume and could do Indian dancing. He asked me if I would do it. I was honored."

The "Illiniwek" name, Dvorak explained, originated with the legendary UI football coach, Robert Zuppke.

"I got the idea from Coach Bob Zuppke," Dvorak recalled in a 1976 interview with a university publication. "Zup often talked to his players about Illiniwek, explaining that the term referred to 'the full Indian man—physical, intellectual, spiritual.'"

Dvorak, who left Illinois in 1934 to become director of bands at the University of Wisconsin, wrote a letter to the recently retired Zuppke in 1941, crediting the coach with helping create the tradition.

Portrayed by Lester G. Leutwiler, Chief Illiniwek makes his first appearance on October 30, 1926.
From the Illio

Lester G. Leutwiler as a young boy.
From the collection of Jean Edwards

"You may recall that I introduced the Indian Chief, Illiniwek, with the Illinois Band, and used the name which you yourself had given. In other words, you named Chief Illiniwek."

In a January 1993 interview with the *Daily Illini*, Leutwiler (who died a month later) remembered how Dvorak had recruited him to portray an Indian for the Penn game.

"Ray called me one day and said, 'Say, I just got a call from Pennsylvania and the football coach out there said they'd send a costume of (Quaker) William Penn to represent Pennsylvania for the halftime show and you fellas try to figure something to represent the University of Illinois," Leutwiler said.

"And I said, 'Well, what's wrong with using an Indian?' Ray fell right in with it."

So at halftime of an otherwise undistinguished 3-0 Illinois win on a chilly, rainy day before 58,861 fans at Memorial Stadium (the biggest crowd in the first season after the great "Red" Grange had left the school), Chief Illiniwek made his debut.

"At the Penn game," Leutwiler recalled years later, "the U of I band marched into the formation and spelled PENN. The Chief ran from a hiding place north of the Illinois stands and led the band with a frenzied Sioux war dance to the center of the field. The band played 'Hail Penn' while the Chief saluted the Penn rooters and Wm. Penn. was impersonated by George Adams, class of 1930 and a U of I drum major. He came forward and accepted the gesture of friendship, and together we smoked the peace pipe in the center of the field. Then we walked arm-in-arm across to the Illinois side. There the band played 'Hail to the Orange.'"

What had been intended as a one-time football halftime show blossomed into a tradition that spanned generations.

The following week the Chief accompanied the team to the University of Chicago, where the Fighting Illini defeated the Maroons. The *Daily Illini* editorialized after the Chicago game that what it, notably, called a symbol "has entitled himself to a place at all football games that the University of Illinois plays. If traditions can be made, the Indian as a feature of the football band should surely be incorporated as an annual symbol of 'the spirit of the Illini.'"

Just how much a tradition the Chief had become was at that time open to debate. A November 14, 1926, story about him in *The News-Gazette* (after his third appearance, an Illinois home win over Wabash College) proclaimed that he "has created a great deal of interest and favorable comment from University and Champaign-Urbana persons." The story and a photo caption repeatedly referred to him as "Chief Illiwek."

But for 80 more years, portrayed by 36 different University of Illinois students (including one woman), at numerous appearances away from Memorial Stadium (including a 1930 halftime show at the Illinois-Army football game at Yankee Stadium), Chief Illiniwek thrilled millions of fans and became one of the most unique and enduring symbols of college athletics.

Tom Kacich is an editor and columnist for The Champaign-Urbana News-Gazette.

Mike Gonzalez (1974-1976) meets Lester G. Leutwiler (1926-1928). *From the collection of Jean Edwards*

THE EARLY YEARS

"As a 16-year-old high school junior, I was invited to *The News-Gazette* High School All-State banquet. To say that I was unsophisticated and naïve would be a gross understatement. … The banquet was held at either the old Tilden Hall or Inman Hotel, both in downtown Champaign. University of Illinois football coach Ray Eliot, who was noted for his ability to inspire young men, was wrapping up his passionate after-dinner speech on Illini history when his demeanor and expression seemed to change as he described the Fighting Illini Spirit. I can't do his presentation justice, but he began to describe how we were not named after a scavenger that lived off of the leavings of others, nor a rodent that lived in the ground, nor a nut that falls from a tree, but after a great and glorious spirit that roamed this land free and brave. He paused, cupped his hand to his ear, and quietly said, 'If you listen real closely, you can almost feel it now.' At that moment, the drummers from the Marching Illini waiting in the hallway hit their drums and the Chief burst into the room. It gives me a little chill even now. To me the Chief was not a college kid dressed up in Indian regalia with war paint on his face. He was that spirit that Coach Ray had just described. Chiefs have come and gone, but the spirit remains as a part of my soul."

Dave Downey
Former UI basketball star and member of the Board of Trustees
from The Champaign-Urbana News-Gazette

Chief Illiniwek Robert Bischoff, 1947.
From the collection of Jean Edwards

WEBBER BORCHERS

By ILLINOIS MAGAZINE

Webber Borchers left his own impact on the Chief Illiniwek tradition. Like Leutwiler, he also had interest in Indian history. Borchers traveled to an Indian reservation in South Dakota to have an authentic Indian costume made. Because of his efforts, he says, he kept the tradition from dying. The university needed something representing pride with the characteristics of the Sioux warrior, he felt. He said he always admired Chief Crazy Horse for the way he managed his cavalry.

So with little money during Depression times, Borchers hitchhiked to the Pine Ridge Reservation. Upon arriving, he found an old woman and two younger women who agreed to make the costume. The old woman helped mutilate Custer's body during the battle of Little Big Horn—or so she said.

Borchers deliberately picked the Sioux because they had a picturesque costume. The Illini tribe could not wear an elaborate headdress because of the trees and brush in the Illinois area. The choice was ironic because the Sioux were bitter enemies of the Illiniwek confederacy.

Besides being the first chief to wear the costume, Borchers was also the first—and last—chief to ride a pony during halftime. He rode bareback around the field, then threw a lance over the goalpost. Bob Zuppke, the football coach, did not like the idea; the horse, he said, did more damage to the turf than band and team combined.

"Well, on one particular day it was raining cats and dogs, and the horses' hooves were splashing mud in every direction," said Borchers. Zuppke took one horrified look and said, 'Get that horse off the field.'" After that, the pony retired. Zuppke was also responsible for Chief Illiniwek's name. It is said that he first used the name in a pep-rally speech.

Excerpted from *Illinois* magazine, December, 1985

Chief Illiniwek A. Webber Borchers, 1929-1930.
From the collection of Jean Edwards

From Webber Borchers
Chief Illiniwek, 1929-1930
written in 1959

I think it is appropriate that a record be made of the beginning of the tradition of Chief Illiniwek of the University of Illinois.

"Leo" Leutweiler, a student at the University, put on an Indian stunt between the halves at the Illinois-Pennsylvania game in Pittsburgh in the fall of 1926. This stunt proved so successful that it was continued as a ceremony and stunt between the halves for the remaining of the year, and until the graduation of Mr. Leutweiler in 1929. The Indian outfit used by Mr. Leutweiler was a homemade one, in which he used turkey feathers.

Webber Borchers of Decatur, also a student, recognized the value of continuing the ceremony as a means of developing an interesting and valuable tradition at Illinois.

In the spring of 1929, he went to Ray Dvorak, head of the marching band of the University of Illinois, and asked him permission to make an Indian outfit during the summer months of 1929, for the use in the fall football season. He told Dvorak that he would take steps to secure the necessary funds to purchase a real Indian outfit that would be the property of the university, and could be handed down from chief to chief, that a tradition could be established. Mr. Dvorak was enthusiastic about this idea and offer, and gave him permission. Webber Borchers prepared the Indian outfit, and used it in the fall of 1929.

In the meantime Borchers attempted to raise funds for the purchase of a permanent regalia during the winter of 1929. He visited nearly every sorority and fraternity on the campus, but without much success, due to the fact that the houses had heavy mortgages, and the Depression was in full sway.

It had been suggested to Borchers by Robert Drake, Scout Executive of the Champaign-Urbana Boy Scout Council, that Mr. Isaac Kuhn might contribute the money for an outfit. When Borchers found that he could not raise the money through the students, hoping to save further work and disappointment he called upon Mr. Isaac Kuhn of Champaign-Urbana, who was very receptive to the idea.

After conversations between Mr. Dvorak and Mr. Kuhn, and possibly Mr. Drake, Mr. Borchers returned to Mr. Kuhn and was authorized by him in the late spring of 1930 to purchase such an outfit for the university bands if Mr. Borchers would personally see to the proper authenticity of the regalia.

In August of 1930, Borchers hitchhiked to the Pine Ridge Reservation in South Dakota, using about 30-some dollars of the money he had collected from sororities and fraternities in the fall of 1929, to pay his way. He carried with him letters of introduction from Mr. Dvorak, of the University of Illinois, and Mr. Kuhn.

Upon arrival at the Pine Ridge Reservation, he contacted the Indian agent and presented to him his letters of introduction and explained his mission. The agent in turn called in a trader at the reservation, and after some discussion, they called in an old Indian woman, who agreed to superintend the making of the outfit. The outfit itself was made by three Indian women, under the direction of the old woman.

In the meantime, Borchers stayed at the reservation for several weeks, but seeing that the outfit would not be completed before the beginning of the school year, it

Former Chief Illiniwek Webber Borchers returns to the field on homecoming November 1, 1980.
Robert K. O'Daniell/The Champaign-Urbana News-Gazette

A. Webber Borchers was the only Chief to ride a horse around the field at halftime.

was necessary for him to leave. This outfit finally arrived shortly before the Army-Illinois game, November 8, 1930, held in the Yankee Stadium, New York City. Borchers wore it for the first time, leading the band down Fifth Avenue, New York, prior to the game.

An interesting sidelight on the old Indian woman, told to me by the Indian agent at the Pine Ridge Reservation was, that she as a girl, had helped mutilate the dead of Custer after the battle of the Little Bighorn.

Chief Illiniwek Robert Bitzer, 1945-1946.
Champaign-Urbana Courier;
Courtesy of the Champaign County Historical Archive,
The Urbana Free Library

Edward C. Kalb, Chief Illiniwek 1935-1938. *From the collection of Jean Edwards*

"October 10, 1942, was up to then the best day of my life. I had talked my father, University of Illinois class of '22, into taking me at age 11 along with him to home-coming weekend. On a golden autumn afternoon, lowly Illinois upset Minnesota, the Midwest football powerhouse. And for the first time, I was privileged to watch Chief Illiniwek dance down the field to Indian war music."

Robert D. Novak
Syndicated columnist
UI alum

Chief Illiniwek William G. Hug, 1951-1952, visits Jimmy Hanner,
a four-year-old from Paris who was unable to attend
a football game because of his polio.

Chief Illiniwek William G. Hug with Chief "Tomeche," 1951-1952. *From the collection of Jean Edwards*

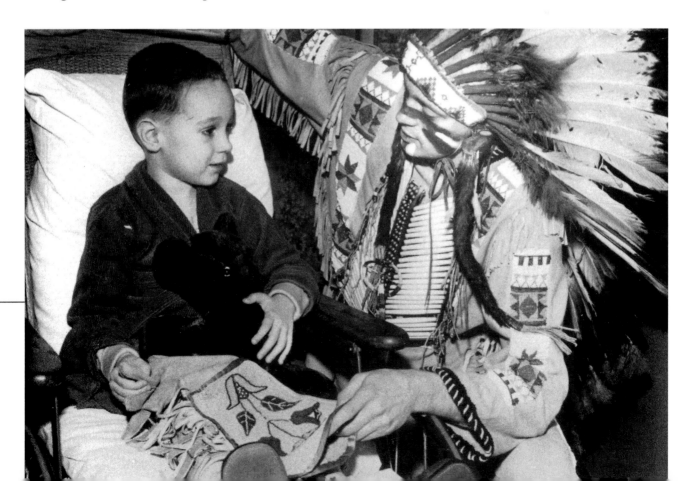

PRINCESS ILLINIWEK

By ILLINOIS MAGAZINE

In 1943 when most of the men on campus were enrolled in military programs, the Chief was replaced by a princess, and the newspaper headlines read, "Squaw takes over while braves go off to war." Idelle Brooks was the first and only woman to represent the university as Princess Illiniwek. Like the former Chiefs, she had previous contact with Indian culture. She grew up on an Osage Indian reservation with her father, a lawyer who dealt with Indian affairs.

She wore a dress with a breastplate and headdress, which weighed about 50 pounds, she said. At the time she was 5-foot-1 and weighed 90 pounds, so she was carrying more than half her weight as she danced the Osage war dance.

Illinois magazine, 1985

Princess Illiniwek Idelle Stith filled the Chief's shoes in 1943.
Harold Holmes/The Champaign-Urbana News-Gazette;
Courtesy of the Champaign County Historical Archive,
The Urbana Free Library

"We have a name up there that doesn't mean a thing to you. Doesn't mean a thing to you. But it means an awful lot to us. We're called the Fighting Illini. And we believe in it. You can't put on the orange and blue spangles of this university without feeling this thing. It was given to us by Red Grange and his gang way back there. Oh, I know it's worth a smile—I know you can look at me right now and say, 'What a guy. What are you thinking about right now? What childish things you've been full of.' Childish? If you smile at this, you're crazy. The Fighting Illini spirit. We believe in it."

Ray Eliot
Illinois coaching legend

Chief Robert Bischoff, 1947.
From the collection of Jean Edwards

"Bob Bischoff stands 6-foot-3 and makes an excellent and impressive Chief. He returned to Illinois after having spent 32 months in the Navy. He became interested in Indian dancing when 13 years old. Some of his most valuable training came from Charles "Eagleplume" Burkhart, who is a member of the Blackfoot Indian tribe and one of the foremost authorities on Indian dancing."
From a contemporary publication by Rawlings Sporting Goods/Photo from the collection of Jean Edwards

Chief Illiniwek William A. Newton, 1931-1934. *From the collection of Bill Newton (C.& S. Photo Service)*

Chief Illiniwek William G. Hug boards the Panama Ltd. bound for the January 1, 1952 Rose Bowl.

Chief Illiniwek Edward C. Kalb, 1935-1938.

Chief Illiniwek No. 3, William A. Newton, in 1934. *From the collection of Bill Newton*

Idelle Stith, Princess Illiniwek 1943.

Chief Illiniwek John Bitzer, 1970-1973

THE MIDDLE YEARS

"Growing up in Champaign, I remember the first time I saw Chief Illiniwek perform. My father was an avid fan and we watched every game we were able to. I almost stopped breathing when I saw Illiniwek's beautiful headdress flowing as he weaved his way through the band.

As their music built to a climax, he jumped straight up out of the band and began that impressive, athletic dance and when he concluded it with that tremendous leap in the air and landed with his arms majestically folded in front of him, my heart almost leapt out of my chest! Ask a 10-year-old girl who looked up into her dad's smiling face if I was demeaned or felt

EVOLUTION OF THE TRADITION

By TOM KACICH

Although in his last years appearances of Chief Illiniwek were carefully restricted to home athletic events, it often wasn't that way before the mid-1970s.

John Bitzer remembers going as the Chief to schools, Scout meetings and athletic department functions at least twice a week.

"I spent twice as much time appearing at nonathletic events as at football and basketball games," said Bitzer, a Collinsville, Illinois, attorney who was Chief for four years, from 1970 to 1974. "It took up a lot of my time."

In a typical appearance, he said, he would meet with a school group and talk about the woodland Indians of Illinois and about the history of Chief Illiniwek. He would take questions and then, using recorded music, would perform the Chief's dance.

"There really were no rules about what you could and couldn't do, at least no written rules. It was whatever Kissinger (Everett Kissinger, the director of the Marching Illini) said the rules were. There was one rule he laid down

that I just finally ignored. He wanted me to return the costume (to the band building) after every time I used it. Eventually I just kept it at my place and took it with me wherever I went. It didn't make any sense to have to get it every time I had an appearance."

Fred Cash, who was Chief Illiniwek in 1964 and 1965, told the *Chicago Sun-Times* that his Chief once marched in Chicago's famed St. Patrick's Day parade at the request of Mayor Richard J. Daley. "He wanted the Chief, and what the mayor wants, the mayor gets," Cash said.

Ben Forsyth portrayed the Chief from 1960 to 1964 and recalled traveling throughout the state to perform and talk to church groups, civic organizations, Scout groups and others about Chief Illiniwek, the University of Illinois and the Indians of Illinois.

John Bitzer as Chief Illiniwek.

Chief Illiniwek Ben Forsyth, 1960-1963.

"I remember going to Springfield and Bloomington and Rockford and Chicago and southern Illinois," he said. "And of course I think I literally went to every small town within 50 miles of Champaign-Urbana. I loved talking about the Illini and the Cahokia tribe. What a magnificent civilization that was. I was in Boy Scouts and I had a scoutmaster who instilled in us a lot of knowledge and an interest in Indian lore. So my talks would always come back to the Cahokia."

Like Bitzer, Forysth said his tenure as Chief was supervised by Kissinger.

But the supervision was light.

"I couldn't perform without his approval so I would tell him who had asked me to appear and where I'd be going, but I'm not sure he ever heard one of my talks," Forsyth said. "It could be really demanding. Let's say I was talking to a group in Bloomington. I'd get out of classes in the late afternoon, hop in my vehicle with my costume, grab a sandwich for the ride over, do my presentation, drive back and get home at about 9:00 and then study for two or three hours. It was a lot of work."

Chief Illiniwek Rick Legue, 1966-1967.
From the collection of Jean Edwards

Chief Illiniwek Fred Cash dances at a football game in November of 1965.
Champaign-Urbana Courier; Courtesy of the Champaign County Historical Archive, The Urbana Free Library

During his time as Chief, Forsyth met Illinois football legend "Red" Grange at an appearance in Chicago, danced the entire length of the Rose Bowl parade in Pasadena, California, in 1964, appeared with Illinois Governor William Stratton at an interstate highway ribbon-cutting and performed at Ohio Stadium when Illinois traveled to Ohio State.

"What I remember about that was Ohio State fans telling me how much better a symbol they thought Chief Illiniwek was than something like Bucky Buckeye or whatever it is, or the Purdue Golden Girl or a badger or some-

thing like that," Forsyth said. "They thought it was so much more meaningful."

Gary E. Smith said that he placed limitations on the Chief's appearances when he took over as director of the Marching Illini in 1976. "I found out that he was going around to all sorts of promotional events. We had calls for him to come to store openings, weddings, funerals, you name it. It was crazy. All of that was gone after I arrived. I finally drew up some written policies and procedures."

Bitzer recalled that while his Chief appeared at every home football game, in those days Chief Illiniwek performed at only about 60 percent of home basketball games. "(Kissinger) didn't want the Chief to be overexposed," Bitzer said. "And there was no way he'd allow the Chief to be at a grocery store opening or something like that."

But Bitzer's Chief was allowed to go with the band to one away football game each year and to the band's occasional halftime appearances at Chicago Bears games at Soldier Field. "Twice I got to meet my hero, Dick Butkus (an Illinois graduate)," Bitzer said. "That was great. He loved the Chief. He thought I was cool and I thought he was cool."

Bitzer's father, Robert Bitzer, was Chief Illiniwek in 1945 and 1946. "My father used to talk to every third grade class in Shelbyville (Illinois) every year about Chief Illiniwek and the Indians of Illinois. His spiel became my spiel," said John Bitzer, who was chosen the Chief while he was still in high school.

Forysth said he made one appearance as Chief that he now questions. "One summer I appeared as the Chief on a float for the Realtors or something like that," he said. "I'm not sure if that was good or bad."

Smith, the former Marching Illini director, said he was shocked by how the university allowed the Chief to be

Chief Illiniwek Gary Simpson in 1968.

used. "I curtailed it immediately," he said. "And there were some key administrators who were not happy about that. But the people in the athletic department were very good to us. They supported us all along, every step of the way.

"But I thought the way the Chief was being used detracted from the dignity of the tradition itself. I didn't think it was right for the Chief to be used as some kind of public relations figure. So the first thing I said was that the Chief could only appear at functions where the band appeared.

"The Chief wasn't like a mascot. It was part of a theatrical, an artistic presentation, like a musical or an opera," Smith said.

Forsyth, 65 years old and living in Great Falls, Montana, said he was distressed that the NCAA pressured the UI to eliminate the Chief's performances. "To me, the Chief represented something that deserved to be instilled not just in athletic teams or at the university but to everyone.

"It certainly was not demeaning or derogatory. The Chief was about greatness. There's a hallway on the east side of the Illini Union that has plaques and pictures of all the great Illini, people who were inventors and business leaders and Nobel Prize winners. Those are modern Illini who represented the spirit of what the original Illini were."

As the Chief became more controversial, his performances were removed from the control of the band. "That was good, because although it was all relatively tame in the beginning, eventually it became very stressful for me," Smith said.

He said he believes the changes he made extended the life of Chief Illiniwek. "If we hadn't made those changes, he would have been gone long ago," Smith said. "I think it brought more of a sense of legitimacy."

Tom Kacich is an editor and columnist for The Champaign-Urbana News-Gazette.

"When I think of the Chief there's one incident that really comes to my mind. I was a leader in the Indian Guide program when my boys were very young. I knew the Chief because he was a Beta and I was a Beta. I asked him if he could come to one of our meetings. He walked in and sat all the kids in a circle, with him in the middle. He talked to all the kids about minding their parents, going to school, doing their lessons and learning to be leaders. They just listened to him talk and took in everything he said, because he was the Chief and they all knew him and respected him. What a great impression he made on these little guys and what a great spirit for the fighting Illini.

I know this memory is far different than the image of the dancing Chief that so many have, but this is what I think of and what I will miss in our community. That's why tears came to my eyes at that last game. The Chief stood for everything good. There will no longer be a Chief to go out and inspire our kids."

Doug Mills
Champaign, IL

Chief Illiniwek John Bitzer at Wiley School in Urbana on November 10, 1970. *Don Brower/The Champaign-Urbana News-Gazette*

These moccasins were handmade by Ogallala clan Sioux Indians on the Rosebud Reservation in South Dakota in 1960. They were proudly worn by Ben Forsyth—Chief Illiniwek at the University of Illinois from 1960 until the end of the 1963-64 football season. This pair of authentic native footwear performed at the Marching Illini halftime shows at Ohio State (1961), Northwestern University (1962), and at Disneyland in California (December 1963). They danced down Pasadena and Colorado Avenues (approximately five miles) during the Rose Parade and at the halftime show in the Rose Bowl on January 1, 1964. These moccasins were retired before the first football game of the 1964 season.
Vanda Bidwell/The Champaign-Urbana News Gazette

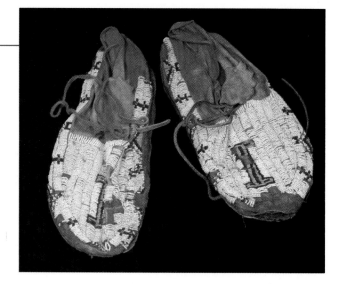

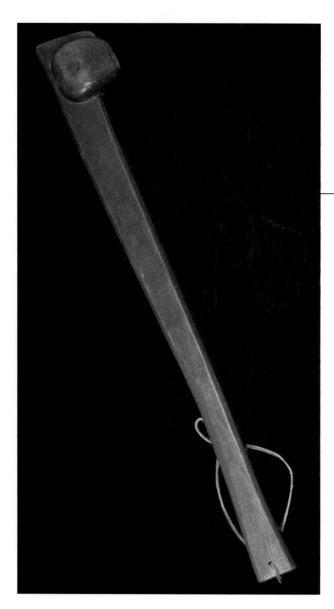

Inscribed: Webber Borchers, Chief Illiniwek II,
Yankee Stadium NY, Nov. 8, 1930
Vanda Bidwell/The Champaign-Urbana News Gazette

"This war club was carried by all the Chiefs from Webber Borchers (Chief #2) until me. In 1963 it was stolen from my Chief costume at Huff Gymnasium after I danced at a basketball game. I spent most of my free time for months trying to locate it. I followed many leads but was never able to find it.

"After I left the U of I and was in graduate school in San Jose, California, my mom, who still lived in Champaign, called to say a guy had come to her door and given her the club. He would not identify himself but said he wanted to return it to the Chief. She asked me what to do with it. She did not know her way around the university, did not know Everett Kissinger (the director of bands), and felt uncomfortable trying to return it herself. I suggested that she hang on to it and I would return it when I got home at Christmas. I forgot about the club and did not see it again for about 20 years."

Chief Illiniwek Ben Forsyth

Chief Illiniwek Matt Gawne,
1977-1979.

MATT GAWNE

"I remember vividly traveling to Champaign with my father and twin brother Martin while in high school to visit my brother Steve and to attend a football game. It was the first time I saw the Chief. I was mesmerized. At that time I had no idea I would be trying out for this coveted honor in the spring of 1977.

"The Illini tradition in our family began with my father, who attended the university before heading to Europe for WWII. As a captain in the Air Force, he flew 50 missions for our great country. He was awarded the Distinguished Flying Cross, Purple Heart and the Air Medal of Honor, which Tom Brokaw described as 'coveted' in his book *The Greatest Generation*.

"My father, who passed away this past March, embodied what it meant to be an Illini. … The Complete Man, The Physical Man, he exuded 'a fighting spirit,' courage, a competitiveness, continually striving for excellence. This is a lesson for all, whether in a game, the classroom or in life.

"You see, it is that 'fighting spirit' that is captured in the dance of Chief Illiniwek, a dignified symbol never to be confused with a mascot.

"A Cuban friend once said to me: *Diga me con quien to andes y te digo con quien to aires*. … This translates to: Tell me who you walk with and I'll tell you who you are.

"I was fortunate to have walked with the men (and one woman) who have represented the noble tradition of Chief Illiniwek—from Lester Leutwiler to Webber Borchers to Bob and John Bitzer to Mike Gonzalez, all of whom deeply care about the dignified portrayal of the Chief and who deeply care about our tremendous institution, and great state. …

"In the 100 times I performed with our world-class Marching Illini to the 76 times I spoke, the audience knew that this tradition was something special. … It was about all that is good with our athletic teams and the university."

Matt Gawne
Chief Illiniwek, 1977-1979

Chief Illiniwek Matt Gawne,
September 9, 1977.
Curt Beamer/
Champaign-Urbana Courier;
Courtesy of the Champaign
County Historical Archive,
The Urbana Free Library

McLEAN COUNTY UNIT #5
105-CARLOCK

Matt Gawne dances during halftime of an Illinois-Centenary game on December 10, 1978.
Phil Greer/Champaign-Urbana Courier; Courtesy of the Champaign County Historical Archive, The Urbana Free Library

Chief Illiniwek John Bitzer (foreground) stands beside his father and former Chief Robert Bitzer on November 15, 1970.

Chief Illiniwek Pete Marzek appears at a backyard bash given by Mr. and Mrs. Stan Ikenberry and Mr. and Mrs. John Cribbet in the backyard of the UI president's mansion, September 6, 1980.

The following was adopted in the mid-1980s by the alums who had portrayed Chief Illiniwek through the years...

THE TRADITION OF CHIEF ILLINIWEK

A Statement of Purpose

From its inception in 1926, the tradition of Chief Illiniwek has engendered pride and respect for the University of Illinois, the citizens and the state of Illinois.

Chief Illiniwek is the representation of the Native Americans who peopled the area now called Central Illinois. Over the years, the tradition has come to symbolize the spirit of a great institution, its students and alumni.

The tradition embodies a spirit of reverence and dignity and as such is a living testimonial to our proud heritage. It also represents the spirit of learning and labor that the founders selected as the motto of the University.

The tradition exists to awaken a higher spirit in all individuals, and to advance the pursuit of excellence.

We are grateful to the many who have played a role in the development of the symbol through the years.

Through the successful embodiment of the "Mighty Spirit" of Chief Illiniwek, we expect to foster a positive image of all Americans and let the tradition be a catalyst to promote their well being.

Chief Illiniwek Peter Marzek, 1980.
From the collection of Jean Edwards

Chief Scott Christensen participates in a parade on October 23, 1981. *Robert K. O'Daniell/The Champaign-Urbana News-Gazette*

King Dad James G. Caprio and Chief Illiniwek Scott Christensen on November 13,1983.
John C. Dixon/The Champaign-Urbana News-Gazette

Tom Livingston, Chief Illiniwek, conducts a class for would-be Chiefs at Memorial Stadium while, in the background, members of the Native American Students for Progress protest, carrying signs into the workshop. Protester Charlene Teters (girl with hat, far right) sits in with the Chief candidates. *Delfina Colby/The Champaign-Urbana News-Gazette*

Chief Illiniwek William Forsyth, 1984-1985. *From the collection of Jean Edwards*

Chief Illiniwek Tom Livingston, 1988-1989. *From the collection of Jean Edwards*

THE MODERN YEARS

"The loss of Chief Illiniwek bears such emotional content that finding the right words is difficult. But what I can say is this: I am baffled that the actions and attitudes of the few have swamped the psyches and passions of the many whose alleged 'trespasses' lay in attempting to honor and revere an illustrious symbol of a great nation of Native Americans whose own courage and valor of long ago inspires emulation even today. I am among the Illini loyalists who cannot fathom faulting our great university for espousing and, yes, demonstrating traditional values on playing fields and courts. Clearly the dance has been ended; but the great spirit of Illiniwek lives on. Long live the Chief!"

Lou Henson
Illinois Basketball coaching legend

Chief Illiniwek John Madigan, 1998-2000.
From the collection of Jean Edwards

"In an era when role models and tradition are fading, the end of Chief Illiniwek is a travesty and another example of poor and inconsistent decision-making in the name of political correctness. … Our Chief had a great impact on my family during our eight years at Illinois. He had no agenda. He affected people of all ages and personified dignity and passion. All through the years the Chief was something people could look up to and take pride in. I am sorry to see such a wonderful tradition legislated against by short-sighted politicians."

Mike White
Retired college and professional football coach

THE LOGO

By JIM DEY

When Jack Davis sees the sports logo for University of Illinois athletics, he feels a sense of pride.

And there's no reason why he shouldn't. Davis, a self-employed graphic artist, created the logo symbol of Chief Illiniwek that has become the national image of UI sports.

"I guess I still have a tremendous sense of ownership. It meant so much for me to do. It meant so much to have the school use it. It's one thing I've really done that met the test of time in terms of design," he said. Davis' image of a Native American wearing an overflowing headdress and breastplate has endured for years and been replicated literally thousands of times, most profitably for the athletics department on university-licensed sportswear.

"It's probably had more exposure than anything I've ever done," he said.

Ironically, Davis' successful logo design was inspired by the University of Iowa's decision to adopt a new logo. He loved the Hawkeyes' sports image.

"I thought, 'What a statement that makes. My school needs something like that,'" he said.

So Davis paid a visit in 1980 to assistant athletic director Vance Redfern, told him what he thought and proposed that he produce a new sports logo for the UI.

"Go ahead, give it a shot," Redfern replied.

It is, of course, much easier to decide to create a new logo than it is to actually create one. What, after all, symbolizes the fighting spirit and tradition the UI identifies with its athletics program?

"That's the dilemma—to condense everything down and come up with a solution that works," Davis said.

He "played around with some different" images, examined photography of American Indians and perused old Illinois sports memorabilia. He ultimately pursued a circular

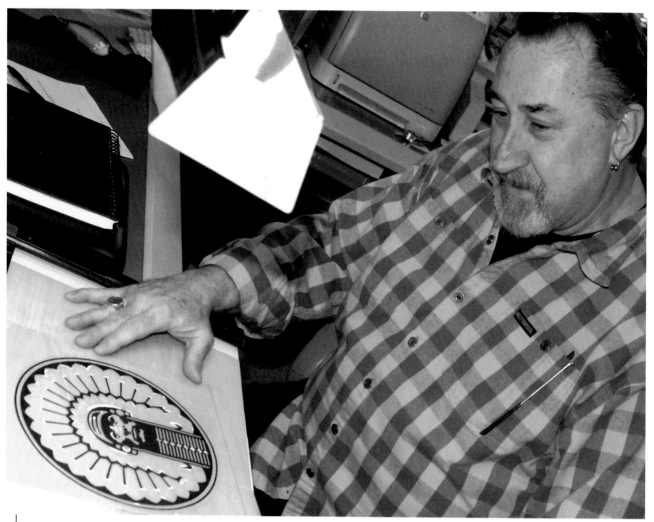

Although he has done much design work since, Davis is best known for his contribution to the Fighting Illini.
Vanda Bidwell/The Champaign-Urbana News-Gazette

theme because "the simple geometry of a circle makes such a nice logo," and it could be shaped by the Chief's headdress.

Within that circle, he included the Chief's headdress, breastplate and a "dignified and stoic" face. By design, there was to be no caricature. "It's a clearly drawn logo. But it has a lot of detail in there. It needed what it had to capture the Chief," he said.

Davis said when he completed the logo, he presented it to athletic departments officials who were "very pleased."

"So that was that," he said. "I just thought it was great to be able to do something that would symbolize the sports program."

They should have been pleased because, as logos go, it is first rate.

Steve Ryan, with VSA Partners, a Chicago graphic arts firm, praised the artwork for its "simplicity" and "perfect symmetry."

"It's a simple, recognizable, powerful mark," Ryan said. "It's something people can get their emotions wrapped around."

For his work, Davis submitted a discounted bill of $210. Since then, he's watched as the logo has been put on wide display and reproduced on all kinds of athletic apparel, generating a mountain of revenue for the UI ath-

Chief Illiniwek Kyle Cline, 2004-2006. *Darrell Hoemann/The Champaign-Urbana News-Gazette*

letic department. More than once, Davis said, he's thought about how nice it would have been to collect a royalty for each item sold that bears his logo. But Davis said that in 1980 sports marketing hadn't really become as big as it is now and that the nature of his trade is "work for hire."

Davis comes by his enthusiasm for the UI naturally.

He was born in Cincinnati, Ohio, but grew up in the Chicago suburbs. He graduated from the UI in 1969 with a degree in graphic arts.

"(Graduation) should have been in 1967. But I got married when I was in school, and it took a little longer," he said.

While attending the UI, Davis not only studied graphic arts, but he played in a rock band. At 61, he still rides a motorcycle and jokes that he has an "artist, musician, biker personality."

Davis was a freshman at the UI when he went to his first home football game at Memorial Stadium.

"I can still remember in the fall of 1963 watching the

Chief come out and just being in awe," said Davis, who remained in the community after graduating and lives in Champaign.

After graduation, Davis worked briefly for the UI, then for himself and then for an advertising firm. He finally went out on his own for good in 1974.

"I like working for myself. I enjoy the freedom of it. I can be versatile with my clients. I have a lot of variety in my work," he said.

After more than 30 years in business, Davis has lots of clients and does all kinds of design work. But among his first clients when he was starting out was the UI's sports department, and one of his first assignments was producing a memorable poster for the 1974 football season.

The poster emphasized the golden anniversary of Memorial Stadium by recreating the image of Fighting Illini football great Harold "Red" Grange, the Galloping Ghost.

Ironically, one of the home games on the 1974 schedule was against the University of California-Berkeley, then coached by Mike White. Six years later, White was the new football coach at the UI, brought in by new UI athletic director, Neale Stoner. Davis said he had the impression that Stoner and his athletic department lieutenants, including Redfern, were looking to upgrade the UI's athletic image.

Davis said that prior to Stoner's arrival there had been "a number of different Indian" symbols representing UI sports and "some of them were not terribly dignified." Prompted by the University of Iowa logo, Davis made his pitch for designing a new department logo and succeeded beyond his wildest expectations.

Aside from the tradition of the now-retired Chief Illiniwek, Davis' logo epitomized the UI's venerated symbol to the world. Of course, along with attacks on the Chief have come criticism of the logo, and Davis has watched unhappily as both Chief Illiniwek and his logo increasingly were mar-

ginalized as the controversy over the Chief continued.

Still, the Chief's image is one that he sees regularly, and it's one that will continue to be on display for years to come. That, Davis said, gives him a tremendous feeling of satisfaction.

"I'm pro-Chief, and I'm pro-logo," he said.

Jim Dey is a columnist for The Champaign-Urbana News-Gazette.

Chief Illiniwek Scott Brakenridge performs at halftime of a UI-Purdue game on October 25, 1997.
Rick Danzl/The Champaign-Urbana News-Gazette

Chief Illiniwek John Madigan, 1998-2000.

Chief Illiniwek Kurt Gruben, 1990-1991. *From the collection of Jean Edwards*

Chief Illiniwek John Creech, 1994-1995. *From the collection of Jean Edwards*

THE CHIEF CONTROVERSY: A TIMELINE

BY JOEL LEIZER, JULIE WURTH AND JODI HECKEL, *THE CHAMPAIGN-URBANA NEWS-GAZETTE*

November 1989—Illinois House passes resolution supporting the Chief, co-sponsored by state Rep. Timothy Johnson, R-Urbana. U.S. Sen. Paul Simon, D-Ill. (above), signs petition calling for elimination of the Chief, inspiring cries of "Keep the Chief, Dump Simon."

October 30, 1926—Chief Illiniwek, portrayed by Lester Leutwiler (above), first appears at the University of Illinois during halftime of a football game at Memorial Stadium.
Photo courtesy of the Champaign County Historical Archive, The Urbana Free Library

November 14, 1989—Chancellor Morton Weir says Chief will stay, calling it a "dignified, respected" symbol.

December 1989—UI orders Department of Agronomy to end its use of "Squanto" cartoon character (right) on its publications.

October 1989—Two University of Illinois students, including graduate student Charlene Teters, member of the Spokane nation, begin protesting the Chief. Teters stands silently outside UI basketball games with a sign reading, "Indians are human beings."

1992—Teters (left) and others form National Coalition on Racism in Sports and the Media, a campaign to ban Indian mascots and symbols.

April 8, 1994—American Indian students, faculty, and staff at the UI file civil rights complaint with U.S. Department of Education, alleging Chief creates "hostile" racial climate on campus."

March 1990—Students for the Chief forms.

October 14, 1994—Campus committee on "inclusiveness," appointed by Chancellor Michael Aiken (right), advises Chief be eliminated. Recommendation is left out of chancellor's final "Framework for the Future" report the next spring.

September 1991—New community group, Citizens for Chief Illiniwek, launches letter-writing campaign to support Chief.

April-July 1995—State legislators approve bill introduced by new state Rep. Rick Winkel (upper right), R-Champaign, making Chief official symbol of UI. But Gov. Jim Edgar (lower right) uses amendatory veto to change wording so that decision rests with the university.

November 1991—Johnson introduces resolution asking UI not to restrict use of Chief.

1990s

December 1, 1995—Department of Education rules that Chief does not violate civil rights of American Indians but urges UI to take "proactive steps" to prevent hostile climate.

October 2, 1991—UI announces Chief no longer will appear in homecoming parade or pep rally.

January 1993—American Indian activist Michael Haney (right) files discrimination complaint against UI with Illinois Department of Human Rights, saying he and others were taunted and jeered for opposing the Chief at October 1992 UI football game. The complaint is later dismissed.

October 11, 1990—After months of protests, UI Board of Trustees votes to retain Chief as official UI symbol by 7-1 vote, with one abstention.

July 15, 1997—Jay Rosenstein's documentary "In Whose Honor?", featuring Teters, is aired on national television, bringing nationwide attention to the issue and accelerating anti-Chief movement.

September 1998—UI professor Stephen Kaufman (left) files grievances against top university administrators, arguing Chief violates UI's own anti-discrimination policies. Trustees and state officials dismiss the complaints.

October 1997—UI homecoming king and queen make anti-Chief sentiments known during festivities. The next year, the UI ends its practice of crowning a homecoming king and queen.

May 1999—NCAA evaluation team visits UI campus as part of certification review. During public input, NCAA team is asked to withhold full certification of UI until Chief is retired.

March 30, 1998—Two new pro-Chief groups form: Students for Chief Illiniwek and the Chief Illiniwek Educational Foundation.

February 16, 2000—UI trustees announce plans for yearlong "dialogue" on Chief and hire former Cook County Judge Louis B. Garippo to oversee process, which costs more than $315,000.

April 14, 2000—Garippo presides over public comment session. After receiving more than 17,000 pieces of correspondence, he issues report in October 2000 that summarizes arguments on both sides but offers no recommendations.

March 9, 1998—Campus faculty-student senate approves resolution asking trustees to replace Chief with new symbol, saying it undermines academic mission; vote is 97-29. Eventually, more than 800 faculty sign petition calling for Chief's ouster.

February 2000—After a visit to campus, North Central Association of Colleges and Schools, which accredits UI, issues report expressing concern about how UI is dealing with the negative effects of the Chief controversy.

July 1997—Alumni Against Racist Mascots forms to show not all university graduates support the Chief.

September 30, 1998—NCAA's Minority Opportunities and Interests Committee calls for end to use of American Indian names and mascots for college sports teams. Statement comes as UI's athletic program undergoes its first certification review by NCAA.

March 1, 2001—Anti-Chief faculty consider contacting prospective athletic recruits and advising them they could be attending a school with a "racist symbol."

March 7, 2001—Trustees respond to Chief dialogue, hiring Chicago public relations consulting firm to help craft their statements. Some trustees talk of working toward compromise.

May 2001—Board of trustees asks trustee Roger Plummer to explore Chief issue to determine if compromise is possible.

January 2002—William Cook (right) of rural Champaign is arrested at Assembly Hall while protesting Chief during UI basketball game. In an e-mail later made public, Chancellor Nancy Cantor says Cook's arrest violated UI policies on free speech. Cook is later convicted of resisting arrest. He and two other protesters file federal lawsuit against UI, claiming civil rights violations by UI police officers and security guards.

March 2002—Plummer presents his report on the Chief to trustees, concluding there can be no compromise.

Fall 2002—UI establishes a Native American House on campus.

August 2003—NCAA Executive Committee recommends schools using Native American imagery do a "self-evaluation" to determine if it is offensive.

Spring 2001—Businessman Roger Huddleston (right) of Mahomet, who produced a film in honor of Chief Illiniwek, co-founds the Honor the Chief Society and pledges to raise $100,000.

April 2001—Peoria Tribe of Oklahoma requests UI stop using Chief Illiniwek.

November 13, 2003—Board of trustees is set to consider resolution by Trustee Frances Carroll to honorably retire Chief and maintain name "Fighting Illini" for athletic teams, but resolution is withdrawn.

March 2, 2001—Chancellor Michael Aiken sends e-mail to UI employees, saying any contacts with recruits must be approved first by Division of Intercollegiate Athletics to avoid violating NCAA rules. Four faculty members and one student sue UI and Aiken, alleging he violated their First Amendment rights, and a federal judge agrees. Plaintiffs are eventually awarded $1,000 each, and Aiken retracts the e-mail in June. Packets are mailed out to 100 prospective recruits.

April 2004—Anti-Chief protesters occupy Swanlund Administration Building for 32 hours. To end sit-in (right), Cantor promises meetings with members of North Central Association during upcoming campus visit and with members of black and Latino caucuses of state Legislature—and that Chief's future will be put on trustees' agenda in June.

August 2004—After an April campus visit, North Central Association issues report saying UI's failure to resolve Chief issue shows failure of leadership and expresses concerns about how controversy is affecting "educational effectiveness" of UI.

November 2005—In a three-month flurry, UI appeals NCAA policy; NCAA agrees that "Illini" and "Fighting Illini" are acceptable but keeps UI on sanctioned list because of Chief portrayal and logo; and UI files second appeal, arguing NCAA exceeded its authority, violated institutional autonomy, and applied policy arbitrarily.

August 2005—NCAA announces policy to ban certain universities, including the UI, from hosting postseason competition because they use American Indian imagery.

April 2006—NCAA rejects UI's second appeal and says university will be subject to sanctions.

June 2004—Trustees adopt resolution calling for "consensus conclusion" on the Chief issue. In later months, they adopt guidelines that include keeping names "Illini" and "Fighting Illini" and considering athletic programs and ability of its athletes to compete at the highest levels.

May 2006—UI is turned down as host site for opening round of NCAA men's tennis championships, despite high ranking of UI men's team.

December 2006—Johnson hosts hearing at Parkland College.

January 2007—Officials discover threats posted by UI students on Facebook Web site against an American Indian student at the UI. A separate posting on anti-Chief site talks of shooting Chief Illiniwek. UI police investigate, but state's attorney declines to file charges, saying postings are protected speech.

February 16, 2007—UI announces Chief will no longer perform and use of name and logo will be discontinued. NCAA announces UI will be removed from list of sanctioned institutions.

February 21, 2007—The Chief (below) dances his last dance at halftime of the men's basketball game against Michigan at the Assembly Hall.

January 18, 2007—Executive committee of Oglala Sioux Tribal Nation asks UI to return buckskin costume and other regalia sold to the university in 1982 for Chief costume.

February 15-16, 2007—Two students who portray Chief Illiniwek sue the NCAA, saying sanctions violate their rights to free expression and academic freedom, and go to court to stop the UI from retiring the Chief. A judge rejects their request for a temporary restraining order against the UI.

May 2006—U.S. Rep. Tim Johnson, R-Urbana (right), and House Speaker Dennis Hastert, R-Yorkville, introduce bill that would allow UI or any other university to sue NCAA for lost revenue if barred from hosting a championship game.

Sources:
The Champaign-Urbana News-Gazette archives and University of Illinois files

Chief Illiniwek Kyle Cline performs at halftime of the Illinois women's game vs. Reebok Lady All-Stars at the Assembly Hall in Champaign on Sunday, November 16, 2003. *Robin Scholz/The Champaign-Urbana News-Gazette*

During an Illinois-Ohio State matchup on October 10, 1998, Chief Illiniwek John Madigan takes the field. *Robert K. O'Daniell/The Champaign-Urbana News-Gazette*

AN UNLIKELY LITTLE CRUSADER

By AMY ECKERT

Until 1989, Jean Edwards was, for all appearances, a passionate but typical Illinois sports fan. Then something happened to make this devoted wife and mother of three abandon the last trace of shyness that she said had haunted her in high school.

That something was a spirited discussion on Jim Turpin's *Penny for Your Thoughts* radio program. There was a movement afoot to get rid of Chief Illiniwek.

"People kept calling him and saying they didn't want the Chief to go," recalled Edwards. "But nobody was doing anything besides talking about it. Somebody had to do something, so I just did it."

And it changed her life.

She started by writing a letter, which she sent to 100 people she felt were "important," asking for permission to use their name in connection with a group she wanted to form called "Citizens for Chief Illiniwek."

"I'm not a political activist," she said. "I don't think of myself that way."

The group started out fairly small, meeting in her home to address and stuff letters. Her children were surprised when people she didn't know began to address her on the street to talk about the campaign. As the word spread, they had to hold meetings at a local hotel in order to accommodate everyone.

A couple years into it, two students formed the Chief Illiniwek Foundation to raise money to support the Chief. When the founders graduated, they asked Jean to carry on the mission of that group, a responsibility that she accepted without hesitation.

Jean had a goal of creating a video about the history of the Chief, which sent her on a mission to collect some serious financial backing. Through those efforts, she was introduced to a local businessman Roger Huddleston.

Jean Edwards reads a letter in her home on September 19, 1991, as she prepares for the "Keep the Chief" campaign.
Delfina Colby/The Champaign-Urbana News-Gazette

"Meeting Roger changed my life," said Jean. "It was like it was supposed to be. We must have talked 10 times a day."

Their combined energy made them a force to be reckoned with. The video became a reality, and the group was renamed "Honor the Chief and the Tradition." They spoke to hundreds of people all over the country about the importance of the Chief. Interest was huge, and the group grew to approximately 1,000 members.

Jean still answers all the mail and fills all the orders for pins, posters and pictures that people place through their web site. She vows she will continue to fulfill that role as long as she is able, and as long as other people remain interested in preserving the tradition of the Chief.

Amy Eckert is director of special projects for The Champaign-Urbana News-Gazette.

"When you burst out of that hidden position into 60,000 people, it is like running to the edge of a cliff and you sprout wings and you soar straight up into a thundercloud. It's awesome."

Tom Livingston
Chief Illiniwek, 1988-89

Cheif Illiniwek Kyle Cline performs after the second Illinois-Northwestern volleyball game on Wednesday, November 12, 2003.
Robin Scholz/The Champaign-Urbana News-Gazette

THE FINAL YEARS

"The NCAA ethicists probably reason that the Chief must go because no portion of the Illini confederation remains to defend him. Or to be offended by him, but never mind that, or this: In 1995, the Office of Civil Rights in President Clinton's Education Department, a nest of sensitivity-mongers, rejected the claim that the Chief and the name Fighting Illini created for anyone a 'hostile environment' on campus. In 2002, *Sports Illustrated* published a poll of 352 Native Americans, 217 living on reservations, 134 living off. Eighty-one percent said high school and college teams should *not* stop using Indian nicknames. But in any case, why should anyone's disapproval of a nickname doom it? When, in the multiplication of entitlements, did we produce an entitlement for everyone to go through life without being annoyed by anything, even a team's nickname?"

George Will
Washington Post Writers' Group
from The Champaign-Urbana News-Gazette

Chief Illiniwek Matt Veronie, 2001-2003.
From the collection of Jean Edwards

Tradition is for the assistant chief (a role added to accommodate demand for the performance at women's sporting events) to dance the last football game each year. The last performance by the Chief in Memorial Stadium was done by Logan Ponce.

Assistant Chief Illiniwek Logan Ponce dances the last performance by Chief Illiniwek at Memorial Stadium at the Illini's final home football game against Purdue on Saturday, November 11, 2006.
Darrell Hoemann/The Champaign-Urbana News-Gazette

Stilling the crowd at halftime, Ponce stands motionless at the 50-yard line.
Holly Hart/The Champaign-Urbana News-Gazette

Ponce continues the Chief's final football performance.
Holly Hart (right), Darrell Hoemann (above)/The Champaign-Urbana News-Gazette

The 20 former Chief Illiniweks gather together at halftime on November 11, 2006.
Darrell Hoemann/The Champaign-Urbana News-Gazette

"I was raised in Montana, and I never thought Chief Illiniwek was insulting to Native Americans. He was not a mascot who ran around the field. He always did his halftime performance in a tasteful manner. If the Illini Tribe still existed, I'm sure a deal would have been struck to retain the Chief, as the Seminoles did at Florida State. Having said that, I can understand and respect what the administration did. But I never felt the Chief was abusive."

Brent Musberger,
ESPN and ABC-TV broadcaster

LAST DANCE

By JODI HECKEL

All eyes of Illini fans were looking upward at halftime of the basketball game, as a video tribute to Chief Illiniwek played on the scoreboard.

Many captured the tribute on digital cameras, then turned to the tunnel in anticipation.

Dan Maloney, who portrays the Chief, emerged to a roar and a burst of camera flashes all over the Hall. At the end of his dance, he started to walk off the court, then turned and went back out to center court and raised his arms again to the crowd.

Maloney's mother, Carol, broke down in tears.

"It just took my breath away, not only his dance, but the way the crowd reacted, all the flashbulbs and everyone standing," she said. "To me, it just goes to show what tremendous, tremendous support Chief Illiniwek has."

The night of February 21, 2007, was an emotional one for Maloney, but he didn't let it show on the court. He expected to be moved by the emotions of the fans.

"It was absolutely incredible," he said afterward. "The crowd reaction was more than I ever expected. I can't express my appreciation.

"I just threw everything I possibly could, every bit of energy into it," he said.

Maren Schuit of Chicago was hoping the atmosphere surrounding the last dance of Chief Illiniwek would be one of celebration, rather than mourning, so "the Chief can go out in style."

Schuit, a 2004 UI graduate, former Marching Illini member, and one of the few women to try out to be the Chief, cried at Maloney's performance, but she was happy to see it.

It was serendipitous that Schuit was able to see the Chief's last dance. She got tickets because her boyfriend

Leading up to Chief Illiniwek's last dance, assistant chief Logan Ponce awes the crowd at the Illinois-Minnesota women's basketball game on Thursday, January 18, 2007.
Darrell Hoemann/The Champaign-Urbana News-Gazette

"My memory of the Chief over the past 22 years has been a little different than most fans. My view of this honored symbol has come from the Memorial Stadium press box and from courtside at the Assembly Hall. Even though the physical presence of the Chief is gone, I will always remember what he stood for. To me, the spirit of Chief Illiniwek will never die."

Jim Sheppard
The Voice of the Fighting Illini

Fans line the floor of Assembly Hall, awaiting the Chief. *Darrell Hoemann/The Champaign-Urbana News-Gazette*

"Please do not slander our Chief by drawing parallels between him and many other Indian motifs. He is the symbolic representation of a much more valuable thought. The modern Chief Illiniwek is many times more meaningful in very positive ways to all who understand him for what he really is. His worth is directly related to Indian culture and mainstream American culture alike, and he is respected for symbolizing the beneficial merging of those two worlds."

Ben Forsyth
Chief Illiniwek, 1960-63

Orange Krush members change their shirts to black once the Chief leaves the floor.
Darrell Hoemann/The Champaign-Urbana News-Gazette

is a Michigan fan, before the announcement that the Chief would be retired.

"These tickets are priceless to me at this point," she said. "Somebody wanted us to be at this game.

"When I was a little girl, they used to show the dance at halftime on TV during basketball games," Schuit said. "My dad would actually get me out of bed so I could watch the Chief dance at halftime, then he would put me back to bed. It makes me sad that my kids will never see the Chief with me the way that I was able to with my father.

"It's something I'm incredibly proud of having been a part of for even a couple of months," she added.

Other fans were in a somber mood.

"It was tough, very tough," said Rick Legue, who portrayed Chief Illiniwek in 1966 and 1967. He teared up watching Maloney's performance.

"This is one of the saddest days of my life," he said. "It's a big, big loss for me personally, and for the community at large."

Many Orange Krush members changed from orange to black at the end of halftime.

"I've grown up with the Chief, so it's really hard for me to realize he's going to be gone," said Kristin Gernant, a UI freshman and Orange Krush member, before the game. "It's going to be a tearjerker, definitely. The (face) paint will be all smudged."

Adam Brown, a UI senior from Decatur, painted the upper half of his body black, with the Chief logo in orange on his chest and "Chief Forever" in white on his back.

"I'm mourning the Chief here, trying to get a little recognition because a lot of students feel the same way I do," he said.

The basketball team also recognized the Chief. During their warmup, the players wore T-shirts that said "The Last Dance" on the front, with the seniors' numbers, and the Chief logo on the back, with the words, "Courage. Honor. Tradition."

Coach Bruce Weber mentioned the Chief in postgame remarks.

"I know it's disappointing for a lot of people," he said. "I hope all the things (the Chief) stands for—courage, strength, bravery, honesty—will stay in the hearts of the Illini Nation forever."

It was an emotional night as well—for different reasons—for Jen Tayabji, co-coordinator of the Progressive Resource/Action Cooperative and an anti-Chief activist.

"It's been a long struggle, and it's long overdue," said Tayabji, who planned to watch the game from home. She said she felt a sense of relief at the Chief's retirement.

"It's a step forward," she said. "It's giving the university a chance to move forward and address issues of racism."

Aaron Dubnow, a UI junior, is a Chief supporter.

"It will be weird to see no Chief next year," he said.

Dubnow is president of the Orange Krush cheering section, which takes a neutral stance on the Chief. While the majority of its members are pro-Chief, Dubnow said there are some who are anti-Chief and others who don't feel strongly one way or the other.

"Hopefully all Illini fans can remember we're still Illini fans and we can support the team, because that's who we really support," Dubnow said. "It's a huge, important game for our NCAA hopes."

As for the halftime performance, Dubnow was watching a little more closely than usual.

"I'm watching the emotions of people around me," he said. "This game is going to go down in the history of Illinois basketball. I want to take in the moment of watching everyone else as well."

The last dance of Chief Illiniwek is performed by Dan Maloney at the Assembly Hall in Champaign, Illinois, on Wednesday, February 21, 2007. *John Dixon/The Champaign-Urbana News-Gazette*

Orange Krush members line up in the waning daylight to attend Chief Illiniwek's last dance.
Darrell Hoemann/The Champaign-Urbana News-Gazette

Dan Maloney performs the last dance of Chief Illiniwek before the crowd. *Darrell Hoemann/The Champaign-Urbana News-Gazette*

"To me, Chief Illiniwek has always served two roles. The first, of course, is it symbolizes and embodies the spirit of the university, the university community, the values, the strengths that the university has. But the other role that some people overlook, but that was very important to me, I think the Chief is an incredible vehicle to bring about interest in learning Native American culture. That was always very important to me."

Scott Brakenridge
Chief Illiniwek, 1996–97

The Orange Krush wait for the Chief to appear. *Darrell Hoemann/The Champaign-Urbana News-Gazette*

The Orange Krush section watches a video of the Chief. *Darrell Hoemann/The Champaign-Urbana News-Gazette*

"We are proud of the fact that no athletic family in Illini history has honored more Chiefs during their athletic careers than the Wrights—Bob, in the 1930s, me in the 1960s, and John II in the late '80s and early '90s. I chose the University of Illinois over roughly 60 school offers for many reasons, and the Chief was definitely one of them. The spirit he demonstrated as a proud man of honor was so much more meaningful to me than some bird, animal, small rodent (gopher) or big rodent (wolverine) or even a nut (buckeye). While I was playing, our Chief, Fred Cash, was actually on the football team. He would leave the field a few minutes before halftime…and emerge then for the wonderful 3 in 1. While recently attending church, I couldn't actually see Christ…but I definitely felt his spirit. … He was there. That is the way I feel now about the Chief's absence. We will look for him—and not see him—but he will be there. The spirit of the Fighting Illini will be on the field. And with the proper leadership, sometime in the future our great symbol for so much good may come back.

"Hail to the Orange, Hail to the Blue, Hail to the Chief."

John W. Wright
St. Joseph, IL

From left, UI students and Orange Krush members Adam Brown, Andy Herichs, Nico Turla, Dan Lundstedt, Neal Kuester painted their bodies to honor Chief Illiniwek. *John Dixon/The Champaign-Urbana News-Gazette*

Chief Illiniwek Dan Maloney, 2006-2007. *John Dixon/The Champaign-Urbana News-Gazette*

"I think it was one of the great traditions in college athletics. I know how much it meant to all the players, all the student-athletes, all the fans, to have the Chief out there performing. I think it's one of the few things in college athletics that keeps people in the stands at halftime. … It's hard not to become a fan of Chief Illiniwek once you get down there and are in the Illini family. You realize very quickly how much that tradition means to all the students, all the alumni and all the fans of Illinois athletics. … You could see the pride and the respect everyone showed to Chief Illiniwek. It was something special."

Ron Turner
College and professional football coach

Orange Krush members take photos of other members before the Michigan game.
John Dixon/The Champaign-Urbana News-Gazette

UI freshman Kari Jackson, left, paints Kristin Gernant's face. Gernant is also a freshman and both are Orange Krush members.
John Dixon/The Champaign-Urbana News-Gazette

"I was a part of the Block I card section committee when I attended Illinois from 1978 to 1982. Being down there on the field at halftime and seeing the Chief up close and personal, bringing unity and team spirit as we sang our school loyalty songs is an experience I will never forget. My sister was an Illinette and we both cried as we watched the final video online."

Ellen Romer
Coppell, TX
from The Champaign-Urbana News-Gazette

"It's been a very humbling and eye-opening experience, being part of something so much bigger than I could ever be. I wish right now I could just freeze time and replay the past year over and over again."

Dan Maloney
Chief Illiniwek, 2006-07

I'M JUST SAD

By JODI HECKEL

The performance at halftime of the final 2006-07 regular season men's basketball game wouldn't look any different.

Dan Maloney, the University of Illinois student who portrays Chief Illiniwek, said he wouldn't use the occasion of the Chief's last dance February 21, 2007, to make a statement, even though some urged him to do so.

But he planned to take more time than usual to prepare. And stick around afterward to talk with band members, see family and friends—and take it all in, one last time.

Maloney's place in UI history as the last Chief Illiniwek is one that never occurred to him when he decided to try out for the position, even though the controversy over the Chief had been raging for years. But then came the announcement February 16 that the Chief would be retired after the last men's home basketball game.

"I always believed in my heart of hearts that common sense would prevail and those in charge wouldn't bow

down to a vocal minority or political pressure," Maloney said.

"I'm just sad. I'm really sad by the whole decision," he added.

He has been inundated with phone calls and e-mails full of emotion and support.

"I think the leadership of the board of trustees has vastly underestimated the extent to which Chief Illiniwek is supported," Maloney said. "The outcry is really going to be deafening."

He first gave serious consideration to trying to portray Chief Illiniwek when he joined the Marching Illini as a freshman.

The new band members were treated to a performance by the Chief at the end of their band camp, and a talk about the history of the tradition. Band members were told they were the guardians of the Chief tradition, because he never performs without them.

Maloney was enthralled.

Current Chief Illiniwek, Dan Maloney, talks to a reporter in his apartment in Champaign on February 17, 2007.
Robert K. O'Daniell/The Champaign-Urbana News-Gazette

"After hearing about how much it means to so many people, that's when I decided I would do whatever I needed to do to be in that spot," he said.

Even being a marching band member felt to him like being a part of UI history.

"You're down in the midst of the (football) field looking up. Everybody is standing up, everybody has got their arms around each other, and they're singing along with the music," he said. "You feel such a privilege to be part of it."

He narrowly missed being named an assistant chief on his first tryout, then made it on his second. When he told his parents he had been named an assistant chief, Maloney said his father didn't believe him at first.

"My mom—she denies this, but I remember this very vividly—she started crying a little bit and got very emotional," he said.

The assistant chief typically performs at the last home football game each season. When Maloney's turn came for the first time, his father and grandfathers were watching.

"Being able to be surrounded by my family at the first football game I performed at is something I'll never forget," he said.

There have been other memorable moments, such as falling and severely spraining an ankle at a women's game last year, but finishing the performance.

Maloney reflects back on the events of the past year. *Robert K. O'Daniell/The Champaign-Urbana News-Gazette*

"You keep going. No matter what knocks you down, no matter what roadblocks are in the way, you have to fight through and finish the performance," he said. "I think that's very applicable right now."

At the first football game in fall 2006, a night game, rumors were swirling about whether this year would be the last for the Chief. Maloney remembers the roar of the crowd as soon as they caught sight of him in the tunnel, and the camera flashes all over the stadium.

His favorite performance during the school year, though, was at the UI-Missouri Braggin' Rights basketball game.

"The fan support, the publicity, the whole atmosphere surrounding it. When you get out there to perform at halftime, the crowd goes nuts, even the Missouri side," he said.

To try to save the tradition, Maloney and the current assistant chief, Logan Ponce, filed a lawsuit against the NCAA and sought a temporary restraining order to prevent the UI from eliminating the Chief. Maloney said being a party to a lawsuit was a very difficult decision.

"I didn't want to put a face on the tradition," he said. "We didn't want to debase the tradition by any means."

But he decided if this was what could save the Chief, he would do it. He didn't want to regret not trying everything.

He'd heard rumblings of an announcement concerning the Chief for about a week and a half before it happened.

"I don't know if I didn't want to believe it or I'd been hearing for so long that the Chief was going to be retired, but I didn't put much stock in it," Maloney said.

February 16 was awful. He couldn't sleep the night before. In the morning, he first heard that the temporary restraining order had been denied. Then he heard about the announcement of the Chief's retirement.

"I just felt sick to my stomach," he said.

But he still held out hope that it's not the end.

"I don't even want to acknowledge that's a possibility right now," Maloney said. "It may seem like the light has gone out, but I believe the spirit of the Illini will live on. A lot can happen between now and football season."

But February 21 promised to be an emotional night for him.

"It's been a very humbling and eye-opening experience, being part of something so much bigger than I could ever be," Maloney said of his time as Chief Illiniwek. "I wish right now I could just freeze time and replay the past year over and over again."

Assistant Chief Illiniwek Logan Ponce performs at halftime of the Illinois-Minnesota women's basketball game at Assembly Hall in Champaign, Illinois, on Thursday, January 18, 2007. *Darrell Hoemann/The Champaign-Urbana News-Gazette*

"You and I were not alive when this wonderful tradition was birthed and I predict the Spirit of the Illini will live after we are gone from this world. What a privilege we have enjoyed to celebrate Chief Illiniwek. Nothing will ever happen to the Chief as long as one person remains alive that knew him. Go Illini!"

Roger Huddleston
President, The Honor the Chief Society

WHAT THE CHIEF MEANS TO ILLINI FANS

By LOREN TATE

If you never experienced Chief Illiniwek as a youth or longtime resident, you may not understand.

If your background happens to be Chicago, Detroit or Indianapolis, or the far reaches of this country, the feelings built from one generation to another in downstate Illinoisans may be a mystery. Recent arrivals on a diverse, multicultural campus don't come easily to the tradition.

Nor are national editorial writers and pundits generally favorable. And yet two of the nation's most respected political wordsmiths, two who grew up with the tradition—George Will and Robert Novak—view the Chief in strikingly positive terms.

"One of America's booming businesses is the indignation industry that manufactures the synthetic outrage needed to fuel identity politics," chastised Will, an Urbana native.

He pointed out that in 1995, the Office of Civil Rights, "a nest of sensitivity-mongers, rejected the claim that the Chief created for anyone a 'hostile environment' on campus."

In words that only Will can muster, he spoke for many when he asked:

"When, in the mulitiplication of entitlements, did we produce an entitlement for everyone to go through life without being annoyed by anything? Civilization depends on, and civility often requires, the willingness to say, 'What you are doing is none of my business' and 'What I am doing is none of your business.' But this is an age when being an offended busybody is considered evidence of advanced thinking and an exquisite sensibility."

Novak called October 10, 1942, "up to then the best day of my life" when at age 11 he attended an Illini homecoming and "was privileged to watch Chief Illiniwek proudly dance down the field to Indian war music."

Chief Illiniwek Matt Veronie at the Assembly Hall in Champaign, Illinois, for an Illinois vs. Ohio State basketball game January 7, 2003. *Robin Scholz/The Champaign-Urbana News-Gazette*

Added Novak: "The accusation that Illinois and other schools degrade Native Americans is absurd. These schools picked Indian symbols in admiration of their valor, ferociousness and indomitable spirit in the face of over-whelming odds. Native Americans were honored in naming states. Illinois is Algonquin for 'tribe of superior men.'"

For Illinoisans who grew up cherishing the four-minute performance of music and dance, it became a brief, imaginary return to the state's heritage. It can be heart-thumping and spellbinding … a semi-religious halftime experience that matched the sincerity of the pregame national athem at University of Illinois athletic events.

Who can explain his deepest feelings to another? An experience that draws one person's devotion may have an opposite effect on his brother. Can we accept our differences?

In this case, as it pertains to UI fans and supporters, the minority ruled. The year 2007 brought an end to eight decades of exhilarating Chief performances. It was for many "a death in the family." Tears flowed. An uncommon number of Illini fans made their unhappiness known through the media.

Many saw the Chief as a link to the past and, with the associated singing of the UI's "Alma Mater," a linked connection to the state university. Described one true believer, "He is a tangible symbol of an intangible spirit filled with qualities a person of any background can aspire to: goodness, strength, bravery, truthfulness, courage and dignity."

The comments poured in:

"He is all men; he is every man."

"I have watched the Chief, first as a child, then as a student and now as a longtime fan and ticket holder. The Chief is in my heart, like a part of my family, and definitely an integral part of the Illini family."

"As I watched Chief Illiniwek, I saw nobility, courage, respect and honor."

Support far outweighed the negative responses. They continued:

"The Chief brings people together. I never put my arm around my dad, but I did when the Chief came out."

"I cried during his last dance. That tells you how I feel."

"He brought treasured memories to so many disappointing football seasons."

"I didn't attend the University of Illinois, but I feel a connection through the Chief."

The feelings cut across age, gender and race. No single issue, not even a hotly contested election, has drawn such feverish debate in and around Champaign-Urbana.

"From the time I was little, the Chief caught my imagination," said another. "He picked up my spirits. I didn't understand the history, but I loved the pageantry. He is a unifying symbol, not like the mascots who parade the sidelines at other schools."

Chief Illiniwek Kenneth Hanks, 1944.
Harold Holmes/The Champaign-Urbana News-Gazette; Courtesy of the Champaign County Historical Archive, The Urbana Free Library

The late Ray Eliot, who retired as Illini football coach in 1959, was perhaps the Chief's most profound spokesman when he delivered a resounding and oft-used speech emphasizing that "the Chief is not a nut (buckeye) or a burrowing animal (badger), but the symbol and spirit of the Fighting Illini."

Put in the simpleist language, Chief Illiniwek should at the very least be deemed harmless by those who don't comprehend. Why would it be different from recognizing without rancor another's religion that you don't agree with? The Chief was never a mascot nor a cheerleader. He was obliquely connected to the athletic event, and he danced for joy and in bringing togetherness. He represented nobility and spirit. The feelings expressed in this performance may have less to do with specific Indian ancestry than with the heritage of the land.

The ironies of the NCAA ruling, that go far beyond Florida State's ability to retain a spear-throwing Seminole horseman, were pointed out by Andrew Cline of the *New Hampshire Union Leader.*

"The Sooners (Oklahoma) were people who illegally occupied land confiscated from the Indians. Oklahoma is Choctaw for 'red people.'

"If North Dakota (which is suing the NCAA) removes Sioux from its jerseys and replaces it with North Dakota, it will still have a tribal name on its jerseys. Obviously, NCAA executives have not thought their plan through.

"The paternalism that comes from intellectual superiority has overruled common sense."

The arguments are nonstop and complex. But for most downstate Illinoisans, and those UI fans who have moved elsewhere, it boils down to "I get goose bumps."

And after years of wrangling, dialogues and confusing consensus, the feeling is strong that if the Chief had to go, he should have been laid to rest like a loving grandfather by those who most respected him. My problem with

the retirement was expressed more than three years ago in these words:

"If thoughtful former board member Roger Plummer, after analyzing the lengthy dialogue and devoting a year to study the subject, concluded it was appropriate to pull the plug, his view would deserve consideration.

"If the great John Cribbet, former chancellor and a Goliath among his law peers, opined that the Chief had become too much of a burden, his argument would be respected.

"If the worldly Stan Ikenberry, who spoke eloquently on the subject during his grand tour as UI president, made a strong declaration, the staunchest Chief supporters would have to stop and ponder.

"But for a Johnny-come-lately to march into this hurricane with slim background and a large agenda, someone who didn't attend the UI, someone who hasn't experienced and doesn't appreciate downstate traditions" … and so on. You get the point.

That particular coup, led by Chancellor Nancy Cantor, failed more than three years ago. But the Chief was ultimately done in by a crossfire of pressures from Indianapolis do-gooders, Chicago politicians and an administration anxious to move forward without the hassle.

Still, Chief Illiniwek continues to hold a strong, peculiar niche in downstate Illinois culture. As a sport figure, he was part of the game experience. As a cultural phenomenon, he sent chills up and down the spines of true believers.

Some can't explain why they feel the way they do. But they know it's good and they didn't want it to end.

Loren Tate is a longtime sports columnist for The Champaign-Urbana News-Gazette *and co-host of several sports talk shows on WDWS radio.*

Chief Illiniwek Ben Forsyth in 1963.
Champaign-Urbana Courier; Courtesy of the Champaign County Historical Archive, The Urbana Free Library

CHIEF ILLINIWEK,
SPIRIT OF THE ILLINI

By ROGER HUDDLESTON

In the fall of 1959, my dad took me to my first Illinois football game. It began a wonderful love affair with the University of Illinois.

The game was against Army, and I marveled at all of the wonderful pageantry and tradition. The most memorable part was when the crowd I was a part of rose to its feet and welcomed Chief Illiniwek. The dignity displayed by John Forsyth, Chief Illiniwek that year, caused a stirring in my soul that I would understand better in the years to come.

To me the Chief was never a specific person. He was a personification of dignity, loyalty, tradition and inspiration that I have come to respect and cherish as I grow older. As a 12-year-old boy, my relationship with the University of Illinois and Chief Illiniwek was nothing more than something I sensed was good. I was just a boy, and the Chief was someone to be revered. When he appeared, everything seemed to stop, no one seemed to speak and the crowds stood in respect. He was different from school

mascots. He wasn't a Chief Wahoo from the Cleveland Indians. He wasn't wild and uncivilized. He wasn't a cartoon that encouraged us to pretend we had tomahawks, like Ted Turner's Atlanta Braves. He was a personification of a noble common heritage; he was a symbol of a unifying spirit that could cause a crowd of nearly 80,000 to become one spirit for a few moments.

He did not speak. He had no opinions. He was not a cheerleader. He was someone you never thought to ask for an autograph. He never appeared at grocery store openings. He didn't hold small children while parents shook his hand. He was "The Chief." He is respected not for the student who portrays him but as a historical individual.

Kara Huffman, a drum major with the Marching Illini, tries to light candles in the brisk wind as UI students and Chief Illiniwek supporters gather in front of the Alma Mater to hold a rally and candlelight vigil on November 12, 2003.
Robin Scholz/The Champaign-Urbana News-Gazette

Chief Illiniwek is each person's opportunity to affirm what is good about the human race. The Chief is the measure of excellence in each of us if we strive for dignity. The Chief speaks volumes when it comes to pride of self, and he never says a word.

The Chief is a unifying factor for a melting pot of people who find common bonds in what is good. He encourages us no matter what the score is, reminding us that our worth as human beings is not determined by the winning or losing of an athletic contest, and he displays the charismatic dignity to be afforded full attention when he appears.

But if the Chief is good, why do other good people object to him?

Why do Native Americans, who have sincere reasons to question every motive behind every portrayal of their ancestors, genuinely object? Why is a student called Chief Illiniwek wearing Sioux clothing and dancing a dance that is not historically correct?

For my position and my advocacy to be valid, I must listen to the concerns with both my heart and my head. To lay one's understanding down and seek truth is to become vulnerable, but sincere effort to attain intellectual honesty and integrity demands this surrender.

I listened to others' opinions and convictions, emotions and passions, legend and fact, bias and resolve, political correctness and moral honesty. My personal mission was to intellectually discover what was and what wasn't. It was to take two steps back and look with my imperfect heart for the perfect answer. I studied what I could, read editorials, essays and papers.

History provided more than I expected. I learned about a vast confederation of Algonquin people made up of many tribes. I learned that these Illini that the French called Illinois were a society of subcultures joined together by a common geographic area and common interests who nonetheless maintained specific tribal differences.

I learned that the confederation came together and, in spite of their diversity, were led by a single leader–a chief.

Today, we are a people defined by a geographic area we call Illinois. We are a society wonderfully blessed by a diversity of subsocieties and subcultures. We are a community that celebrates things right and condemns things wrong. What better symbol to represent all we cherish and hope for than a human being with character qualities we all treasure and hold as the measure of character?

What better symbol than one with historical significance who shares identity with our home state of Illinois?

What better symbol of dignity, loyalty, tradition and inspiration can represent us all in a world still populated by a people who fall short of perfection?

It is to these ideals I reaffirm my commitment to the Illiniwek Tradition.

Roger Huddleston is president of the Honor the Chief Society (www.honorthechief.org).

Kenneth Hanks performs as Chief Illiniwek at a home football game September 23, 1944. The dog was not part of the performance. Harold Holmes/The Champaign-Urbana News-Gazette; Courtesy of the Champaign County Historical Archive, The Urbana Free Library

THE CHIEFS

1926–1928 **Lester Leutwiler**

1929–1930 **A. Webber Borchers**

1931–1934 **William A. Newton**

1935–1938 **Edward C. Kalb**

1939–1940 **John Grable**

1941–1942 **Glenn Holthaus**

1943 **Idelle Stith Brooks**

1944 **Kenneth Hanks**

1945–1946 **Robert Bitzer**

1947 **Robert Bischoff**

1948–1950 **James A. Down**

1951–1952 **William G. Hug**

1953–1955 **Gaylord "Dean" Spotts**

1956 **Ronald S. Kaiser**

1957–1959 **John W. Forsyth**

1960–1963 **Ben Forsyth**

1964–1965 **Fred Cash**

1966–1967 **Rick Legue**

1968–1969 **Gary Simpson**

1970–1973 **John Bitzer**

1974–1976 **Mike Gonzalez**

1977–1979 **Matt Gawne**

1980 **Pete Marzek**

1981–1983 **Scott Christensen**

1984–1985 **William Forsyth**

1986–1987 **Michael Rose**

1988–1989 **Tom Livingston**

1990–1991 **Kurt Gruben**

1992 **Steve Raquel**

1993 **Jeff Beckham**

1994–1995 **John Creech**

1996–1997 **Scott Brakenridge**

1998–2000 **John Madigan**

2001–2004 **Matt Veronie**

2004–2006 **Kyle Cline**

2006–2007 **Dan Maloney**

"I will always remember making my first trip to see Illinois play a Mike White-coached California team. The Illini weren't particularly good then. We got beat. But at halftime, no one was leaving the stands, wasn't it time to go get something to eat? Dad told me we'd wait, 'he' was going to be coming out any moment.

"And then there 'he' was. Chief Illiniwek emerged from the middle of the Marching Illini to the thunderous roar of 60,000-plus people and as he performed the crowd seemed to be lifted. All eyes on him, the Chief incited the place into a near frenzy. Clapping along and then raising their arms with the Chief as he stopped at midfield.

"Then the roaring crowd became dead silent. Everyone began to sing the "Alma Mater." Arms linked around shoulders and swaying, 60,000 strangers came together as one, all due to the solitary figure in the center of the field. The song ended, and the Chief began his athletic dance performance again to the absolute delight of the entire stadium.

"And then that was that. Off with the band. No parading around the sidelines. No stunts with the cheer-leaders. Definitely no shenanigans that come with a regular mascot. No, this was something special."

Kent Stock
Arthur, IL
from The Champaign-Urbana News-Gazette

Remember the Chief Forever

The honored symbol of the University of Illinois for over 80 years, Chief Illiniwek performed for the last time at the Fighting Illini's final men's home basketball game of the season on Wednesday, Feb. 21.

By popular demand, a variety of commemorative Chief Illiniwek posters are now available for purchase.

Chief Front Page
(18" x 24")

$10 each
(price includes tax)

The News-Gazette®

Last Dance at Illini Football $30 each

(price includes tax)

The **Last Dance at Illini Football** poster is an 18" x 24" **Limited Edition** poster with a run of 1,000. Each of these "Last Dance" posters is hand numbered and includes a certificate of authenticity.

The Chief Illiniwek Tradition (18" x 24")

$10 each (price includes tax)

Order your posters online at www.news-gazette.com/chief

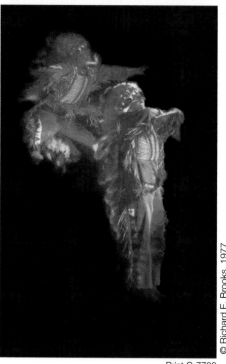

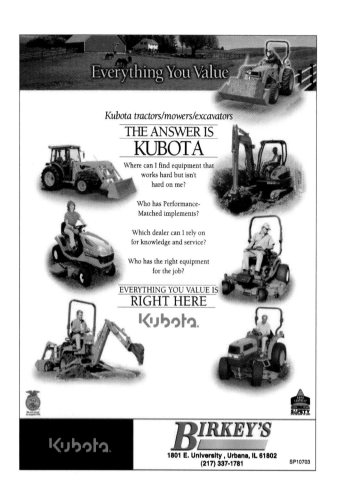
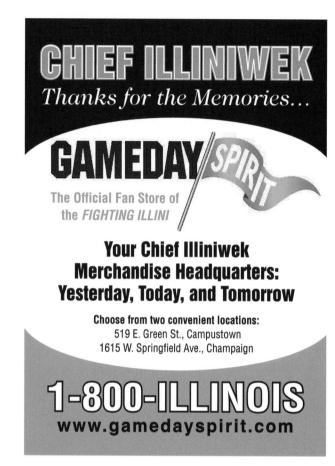

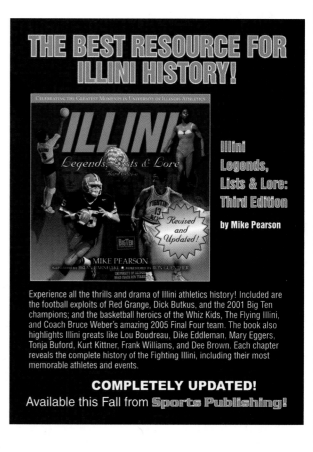

Celebrate the Heroes of Illinois Sports in These Other Releases from Sports Publishing!

A Century of Orange and Blue

This in-depth and photo-filled look at the history of one of college basketball's premier programs is full of fond memories of fantastic teams and the amazing players and coaches that put Illini basketball on the national map. *A Century of Orange and Blue* details everything from the Whiz Kids of 1942 to the Flying Illini of 1989.

ISBN: 1-58261-793-7
$29.95 hardcover

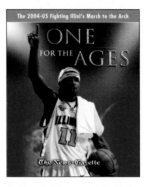

One for the Ages: The 2004-05 Fighting Illini's March to the Arch

Full of vibrant full-color photos from *The News-Gazette* in Champaign, this book takes readers through the amazing regular and post-seasons for the top-ranked Fighting Illini, including their unforgettable run to the National Championship game.

ISBN: 1-59670-132-3 • $19.95 (hardcover)
1-59670-134-X • $14.95 (softcover)

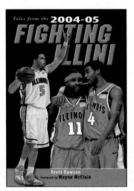

Tales from the 2004-05 Fighting Illini

The never-to-be-forgotten season is captured step-by-step on the magical "March to the Arch," with insights and new perspectives into what made the team so special, an examination into their funny bone, and a look at their fierce will to win. The entire season was a rollercoaster ride of emotion, relive it with this book.

ISBN: 1-59670-121-8
$19.95 hardcover

Glory Days: Legends of Illinois High School Basketball

Among the many high school basketball legends covered in *Glory Days Legends of Illinois High School Basketball* are Mannie Jackson, now the owner of the Harlem Globetrotters, and Quinn Buckner, now an executive with the Indiana Pacers. This book covers Illinois high school basketball like no other book ever published.

ISBN-10: 1-58261-945-X
ISBN-13: 978-1-58261-945-3 • $14.95 softcover

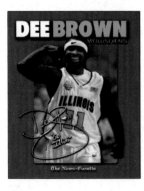

Dee Brown: My Illini Years

The daily newspaper that covered Dee Brown more than any other, *The News-Gazette* in Champaign, highlights his four seasons at the University of Illinois through numerous articles and stories, along with dozens of vibrant full-color photos. The book also features tribute sections, an epilogue from Coach Bruce Weber, and quotes from teammates, coaches, and UI fans.

ISBN: 1-59670-171-4
$14.95 softcover

Entangled in Ivy: Inside the Cubs' Quest for October

Readers are taken behind the management philosophies and inside the Cubs' clubhouse in this unique book. The Cubs' unbelievable situation is detailed in the words of the front office, the many managers, and the players themselves.
2007 release!

ISBN-10: 1-59670-189-7
ISBN-13: 978-1-59670-189-2
$16.95 softcover

All books are available in bookstores everywhere!
Order 24-hours-a-day by calling toll-free **1-877-424-BOOK (2665)**.
Also order online at **www.SportsPublishingLLC.com**.